Food for Healthy Teeth

by Helen Frost

Consulting Editor:
Gail Saunders-Smith, Ph.D.

Consultant:
Karen Masbaum Yoder, RDH, Ph.D.
Indiana University
School of Dentistry

Pebble Books

an imprint of Capstone Press
Mankato, Minnesota

Pebble Books are published by Capstone Press
151 Good Counsel Drive, P.O. Box 669, Mankato, Minnesota 56002
http://www.capstone-press.com

2 3 4 5 6 05 04 03 02 01

Library of Congress Cataloging-in-Publication Data
Frost, Helen, 1949–
    Food for healthy teeth/by Helen Frost.
    p. cm.—(Dental health)
    Includes bibliographical references and index.
    Summary: Lists foods that make teeth strong.
    ISBN 0-7368-0113-8
    1. Nutrition and dental health—Juvenile literature. [1. Nutrition 2. Teeth—Care
and hygiene.] I. Title. II. Series: Frost, Helen, 1949– Dental health.
    RK281.F76 1999
    617.6′01—DC21   98-4147
                                                                      CIP
                                                                      AC

Note to Parents and Teachers

This series supports the health education standards for how to maintain personal health. This book describes foods that are healthful for teeth. The photographs support emergent readers in understanding the text. Repetition of words and phrases helps emergent readers learn new words. This book introduces emergent readers to vocabulary used in this subject area. The vocabulary is defined in the Words to Know section. Emergent readers may need assistance in reading some words and in using the Table of Contents, Words to Know, Read More, Internet Sites, and Index/Word List sections of the book.

Table of Contents

Healthy foods make
teeth strong.

Milk makes teeth strong.

8

Eggs make teeth strong.

Carrots make teeth strong.

Nuts make teeth strong.

14

Strong teeth bite apples.

Strong teeth chew pizza.

Strong teeth crunch popcorn.

Healthy teeth help you eat healthy food.

Words to Know

carrot—a long, orange vegetable; the part of a carrot that people eat grows underground.

crunch—to crush or chew something noisily

healthy—well and strong; eating good foods makes teeth healthy.

strong—powerful and hard to break; people with strong teeth can easily bite and chew food.

Read More

Gillis, Jennifer Storey. *Tooth Truth: Fun Facts and Projects.* Pownal, Vt.: Storey Communications, 1996.

Hausherr, Rosmarie. *What Food Is This?* New York: Scholastic, 1994.

Kalbacken, Joan. *The Food Pyramid.* A True Book. New York: Children's Press, 1998.

Internet Sites

Healthy Teeth
http://www.healthyteeth.org

Snack Facts
http://www.umanitoba.ca/outreach/wisdomtooth/snack.htm

Your Diet and Dental Health
http://www.ada.org/public/topics/diet.html

Index/Word List

Word Count: 40
Early-Intervention Level: 6

Editorial Credits
Colleen Sexton, editor; Clay Schotzko/Icon Productions, cover designer;
    Sheri Gosewisch, photo researcher

Photo Credits
Craig D. Wood, 8, 20
David F. Clobes, 12
Mary E. Messenger, 6
Nancy Ferguson, 10
Shaffer Photography/James L. Shaffer, 4, 16
Unicorn Stock Photos/Tom Edwards, cover; Joel Dexter, 18
Uniphoto/Kathy Ferguson, 1; David M Doody, 14

24